ANCIENT CIVILIZATIONS

West African Kingdoms

By Julie Nelson

Steadwell Books

Raintree Steck-Vaughn Publishers

A Harcourt Company

Austin · New York

www.steck-vaughn.com

Published by Raintree Steck-Vaughn Publishers, an imprint of Steck-Vaughn Company.

Library of Congress Cataloging-in-Publication Data
  West African Kingdoms/by Julie Nelson.
      p.cm.—(Ancient civilizations)
  Includes bibliographical references and index.
  ISBN 0-7398-3581-5
      1. Ghana Empire--Juvenile literature. 2. Mali Empire--Juvenile literature.
3. Songhai Empire--Juvenile literature. 4. Africa, Sub-Saharan—Civilization--Juvenile literature. 5. Africa, Sub-Saharan--History--To 1884. [1. Ghana Empire.
2. Mali Empire. 3. Songhai Empire. 4. Africa, Sub-Saharan—Civilization.
5. Africa, Sub-Saharan--History.] I. Title. II. Ancient civilizations (Raintree Steck-Vaughn)
DT352.65 .N45 2001
967'.02—dc21

                                                                    2001019828
Printed and bound in the United States of America
1 2 3 4 5 6 7 8 9 10 WZ 05 04 03 02 01

Produced by Compass Books

Photo Acknowledgments
Corbis, cover, title page, 4, 6, 9, 10, 15, 16, 19, 20, 29, 30, 32, 36, 43
Digital Stock, 25

Content Consultants
Dr. Kenneth Wilburn
Department of History
East Carolina University
Greenville, North Carolina

Don L. Curry
Educational Author, Editor, Consultant, and Columnist

Contents

Many of Africa's first settlements formed along rivers like this one, the Niger River.

About Ancient Africa

From about A.D. 500 to 1700, great kingdoms famous for gold and learning formed in West Africa. Some of these well-known kingdoms became the **empires** of Ghana, Mali, and Songhay. Their kings set up central governments to control their people and land. They also opened schools, built large cities, and had programs to take care of the poor.

African kingdoms often started in places where people could find water and good land for farming. This limited the number of places where people could settle. The best soil for farming was often near Africa's rivers. Many people lived in cities along the rivers. They fished, farmed, and raised animals.

▲ This camel caravan is crossing the Sahara
Desert in the same way as ancient caravans.

Early People and Trade

The people of **ancient** Africa lived in small
family groups called **clans**. Each clan built a
small village and had a ruler. Many clans lived
inside areas of land called kingdoms. Many
kingdoms joined to form empires ruled by
one king. As empires grew larger, some
villages grew into large cities.

People in different kingdoms traded goods with each other. Traders made roads or trails through the Sahara Desert. The Sahara Desert separates the northern African countries from the rest of Africa. These roads or trails are called trade **routes**. Trade routes led to important trading cities.

Traders carrying goods from as far away as China led herds of camels across the desert. A group of camels and traders is called a **caravan**.

Traders carried mostly salt and gold along the trade routes. They took salt from mines in northern Africa and traded it for gold mined from other parts of Africa. West Africans used gold for decoration. But it was not as important to them as salt. That is because the climate in West Africa can be very hot. In hot weather, people lose the salt in their bodies when they sweat. People need salt to live. West African people needed salt so much that it was sometimes worth as much as the gold they mined from their land.

Religion

Religion shaped many early African kingdoms. Different clans had different religions. Kings were in charge of a clan's religion. Most clans believed there were spirits in all things. For example, trees, animals, and rocks each had their own spirit. Many Africans also worshiped the spirits of their dead family members.

During A.D. 600 and 700, Arab ways of life spread across North Africa and south along the Saharan trade routes. These North African Arab traders brought the religion of Islam to West African people. People who practice Islam are called **Muslims**. Muslims believe in one god called **Allah**.

Islam was started by an Arabian man named Mohammed. He was born in **Mecca**, a city in Saudi Arabia. Mecca is the center of the Islamic religion. Muslims try to make a **pilgrimage** to Mecca at least once in their lifetime. A pilgrimage is a trip taken for a religious reason.

Many modern Muslims still make pilgrimages to holy places like this one in Mecca.

Islam and native African religions sometimes existed together peacefully. To please Muslim traders, many African kings followed some Islamic practices, but they also practiced native African religions. Some African people chose to become Muslims. Some large cities had separate areas for Muslim Africans.

This ancient African book was written in Arabic by a Muslim scholar.

How Do We Know?

There are several ways we know about early Africa. From 600 A.D. Muslim traders wrote books and letters about life in the African cities they visited. A few African people also wrote the history of their people in Arabic.

Archaeologists are scientists who study the past. They search for **artifacts**. Artifacts are things made or used by people in the past. Archaeologists have found African artifacts. They have also found the remains of houses and cities. Archaeologists study these things to find out how people once lived.

Griots are one of the most important ways people know about the past. Griots are African storytellers. They learn long **epics**, or poem-like stories about the past, and repeat them to other people. Griots sometimes play music, sing, and dance when they tell stories. People of early Africa did not write down their history. Instead, every clan and every king had a griot. It was the griot's job to remember the events that happened and pass them down to children. Griots in modern Africa still tell stories about Ghana, Mali, and Songhay.

**GHANA
EMPIRE**

AFRICA

Timbuktu

Kumbi Saleh

Gao

Jenne

Niani

*Lake
Chad*

LEGEND

Ghana Territory

Surrounding land

Cities

Water

*Atlantic
Ocean*

The Empire of Ghana

Around the eleventh century, travelers wrote about an amazing land in West Africa. The land was Ghana, and its king was so powerful that people threw dust on their heads as they bowed before him. Ghana was the first of three great empires in West Africa.

At its height, Ghana covered about 250,000 square miles (647,497 square km) between the Niger and the Senegal Rivers. Ghanaians controlled this area for about 300 years, until A.D. 1235.

About Ghana

The Soninke people built the Ghana Empire from their original homeland, Wagadu. They spoke a language called Mande. Later, the Soninke kings ruled over many different groups of people. Most of these groups spoke their own languages and had their own ways of life. The kings collected large **tributes**, or payments, from the people they ruled. Kings also sent soldiers to protect their **subjects**.

When Ghana was at its most powerful, the king could raise an army of about 200,000 soldiers. The king called on these extra soldiers in times of war. He also had a regular army of professional soldiers who helped him keep control of his empire. The soldiers also kept trade routes safe from thieves.

Ghana's army was stronger than the armies of other kingdoms because its soldiers fought with iron weapons. Many of Ghana's neighbors and enemies fought with weaker weapons made of stone, bone, or wood.

This ancient African spear tip is made of iron.

Special drummers played drums like these whenever they followed the king.

Kings of Ghana

Griots tell about the first king of Ghana. He came from the east and founded the main city of Kumbi Saleh. The Soninke believed that all their kings and other ruling families **descended** from this first king.

Kings were all-powerful in Ghana. The people worshiped, or served, them like gods.

Kings were leaders of Ghana's religion and army. The kings walked around Kumbi Saleh followed by special drummers and wise men. If any of the king's people had disagreements, the king decided who was right or wrong.

Kings had help running Ghana. They divided the kingdom and put a governor in charge of each part. The governors made sure things ran smoothly. Kings also had help in the places they conquered. When they took over a new place, they let the **local** ruler stay in charge. The ruler had to obey the king and pay tribute.

People worshiped their kings even in death. The Soninke believed kings went to the afterlife when they died. They buried their kings in a special forest where only **priests** could go. A priest's job is to serve the gods. Priests made a wooden house for each king's body. They placed clothes, weapons, riches, and food in the house for the king's afterlife. Finally, the priests made a large dirt pile over the house.

Trade

Ghana was so rich that people north of the Sahara nicknamed it the land of gold. It became rich because it controlled the flow of gold and salt. People mined salt in Taghaza, north of Ghana. People mined gold in Bambuk, south of Ghana. Traders had to pass through Ghana to trade salt for gold. Each time they traveled through Ghana, traders paid taxes in gold to the king. A tax of this type is called a **tariff**. In return, the king ordered his army to keep traders safe from thieves.

Goods passed all the way from Ghana to Egypt, Europe, and the Middle East. Traders carried copper, ivory, honey, dried fruit, kola nuts, food, and slaves through Ghana.

Because the gold mines were so important, only a few people knew where they were. To keep this secret, the miners started a special way of trading. The traders went to a special meeting place and beat a drum. They placed the goods they wanted to trade on the ground. They then left. Miners came and put

▲ These men are digging salt chunks out of the ground just as ancient Africans did.

bags of gold dust next to the goods. Then they beat the drum and left. The traders came back and looked at the gold. If it was enough, they took it and left. If they wanted more gold, they beat the drum and left again. The miners either added more gold or decided that they did not want to trade.

▲ This modern village in Ghana has a wall surrounding it like ancient villages did.

People

Each person in Ghana belonged to a clan. Every clan did a special job. Some clans were farmers, while others made cloth. Clan members lived and worked together in compounds. Inside the compounds, people built small, round homes made of mud or stone. Homes were covered with grass roofs. A short wall surrounded the compound and helped keep out wild animals.

The Kante was one of the most important clans. Kante men were blacksmiths. A blacksmith is a person who makes things out of metal. The Kante did not share their secret skills with other clans. They made the iron weapons and tools that gave Ghana so much power. Some people feared the Kante because they thought blacksmiths had magic powers.

Most people in Ghana were farmers. Their iron tools helped them grow extra crops for trading. Common crops were grains, such as millet and sorghum. Farmers also grew cotton, rice, pumpkins, and watermelons.

Both men and women worked hard. The men hunted, fished, and served in the king's army if there was a war. Women gathered crops and made food and **pottery**. Pottery is something made from clay, such as a bowl.

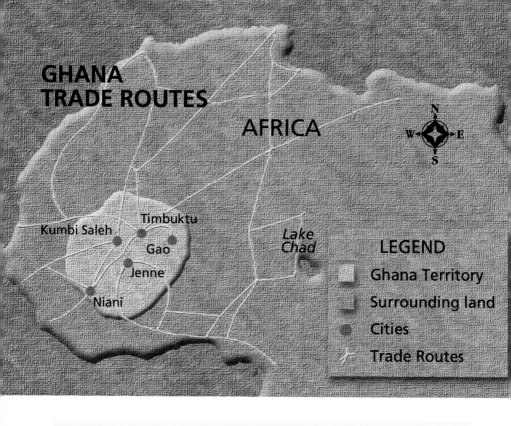

GHANA
TRADE ROUTES

AFRICA

N
W◆E
S

Timbuktu

Kumbi Saleh
Gao

Lake
Chad

LEGEND

Jenne

Ghana Territory

Niani

Surrounding land

Cities

Trade Routes

Caravans that traveled along the trade routes
often stopped in Kumbi Saleh.

The Capital City

About 15,000 people lived in Kumbi Saleh,
the capital city of Ghana. A capital is the
center of government.

The city was divided into two parts. They
were about 6 miles (9.6 km) apart from each
other. The king and the native African people

lived on one side of the city. Because this part of the city was surrounded by woods, it was called Al Khaba, meaning the forest. A tall, thick wall also surrounded the king's half of the city.

The king's house was the largest house in Al Khaba, but it was built in the same style as common people's houses. It was round and had a grass roof. Many small houses surrounded the king's house. The king's wives, children, and government workers lived in these houses.

Kumbi was the Muslim half of Ghana's capital. Muslim traders, lawyers, religious leaders, and teachers lived there. They lived in rectangle-shaped stone houses. Richer people lived in houses with two levels and up to nine rooms. Kumbi also had 12 **mosques**. A mosque is a Muslim house of worship. The city had schools and a huge market. People came from all around Ghana to buy the many goods for sale in Kumbi's huge market. People bought things such as horses, cloth, swords, books, jewelry, silk, and rare birds.

Clothing

Because of the heat, people wore clothing that was simple, light, and loose. They wrapped pieces of cotton cloth around their bodies. They also wrapped their heads in pieces of cloth called turbans.

The king was the only person allowed to wear clothes that were sewn. His clothes were made of colorful silk with gold threads woven into it.

What Happened to Ghana?

Near the end of the Ghana Empire, there was a seven-year drought. A drought is a long period with no rain. Crops died and people did not have enough food to eat. Many people left Ghana. At the same time, in the 1050s, Muslim warriors from Morocco attacked Ghana. These Muslims were called Almoravids.

The drought and attacks by the Almoravids made Ghana weak, but it did not fall completely. However, Ghana's king was no

A seven-year drought dried up Ghana's land.
People could not grow enough crops to eat.

longer powerful enough to control the salt
and gold trade. The people that he had ruled
broke up into their own kingdoms. Kings in
these new kingdoms fought for power and
began to take over the trade routes. When
this happened, the Ghana Empire became a
small kingdom once again.

**MALI
EMPIRE**

AFRICA

Timbuktu

Kumbi Saleh

Gao

Jenne

Niani

*Lake
Chad*

LEGEND

N
W   E
S

Mali Territory

Surrounding land

Cities

Water

*Atlantic
Ocean*

The Empire of Mali

About 150 years after the Ghana Empire fell, a new empire rose to power in West Africa. Sundiata was a Mandinka ruler who united all the kingdoms that had split apart after Ghana fell. The new empire he built was called Mali.

Mali was one of the strongest empires of the 14th century. It spread from its capital city of Niani on the Niger River until it was about three times larger than Ghana had been. At the time, Mali was known as the richest land with the richest king. It controlled the salt and gold trade of West Africa from A.D. 1200 to 1500.

About Mali

Sundiata made sure that Mali had a better food supply than Ghana. He used his army to clear new farm fields and plant crops. Mali became a rich farming area. Because Niani was next to the river, the people of Mali used the river to move goods around their kingdom. Farmers used boats to send food to large cities. Because of this, people could move to cities and still have enough food to eat.

Mali's cities were famous. Timbuktu, Gao, and Jenne became important centers of trade and learning. Muslims from around the world traveled to these cities to study.

Kings of Mali

Mali was like Ghana in many ways. However, the kings of Mali were called **mansas**. Like the kings of Ghana, mansas divided the empire into parts and put a governor in charge of each part. Mansas also had advisors. Advisors gave the mansas advice on how to rule the empire. Each advisor was

Kings had to cross the Sahara Desert to reach Mecca.

also in charge of something. For example, the hari farma was in charge of fishing, while the babili-farma **organized** farming.

Unlike Ghana's kings, mansas were mostly Muslim. The mansas made pilgrimages to the holy city of Mecca. To reach Mecca, kings joined caravans and traveled across the Sahara Desert along one of the trade routes.

Musa brought back people from his pilgrimage to help him build mosques like this one.

Mansa Musa

The most famous king of Mali was Mansa Musa. Musa ruled for 25 years. Some archaeologists believe he doubled the size of Mali and tripled the amount of trade.

Musa made a famous pilgrimage to Mecca in 1324. Some stories say his caravan had about 60,000 people, including princes and army leaders from the different kingdoms he ruled. Musa took these people so they could not take over the empire while he was away. He also brought 500 slaves who walked holding large staffs, or sticks, made of pure gold. One hundred camels carried 300 pounds (136 kg) of gold. Another 100 camels carried food, clothes, and supplies.

As he traveled, Musa amazed people with his kindness and riches. He gave away so much gold that he had to borrow money for the trip back to Mali.

Musa learned many new things on his pilgrimage. He brought these ideas back with him to Mali. Teachers, writers, scientists, and builders from Egypt and other countries came back with Musa. These people helped him build large mosques and start courts of law and famous schools all around Mali.

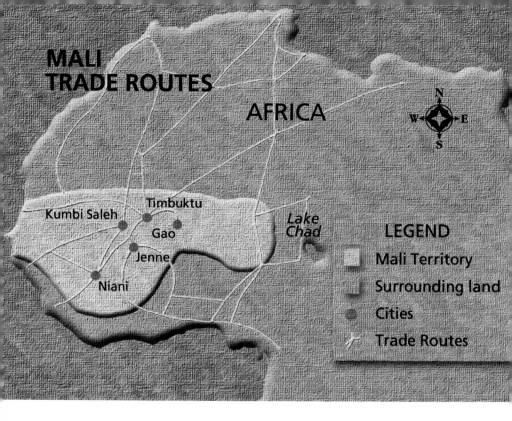

MALI TRADE ROUTES

AFRICA

Kumbi Saleh

Timbuktu

Gao

Jenne

Niani

Lake Chad

LEGEND

Mali Territory

Surrounding land

Cities

Trade Routes

> ⬆ This map shows where the trade routes were when the Mali Empire ruled.

Trade

Mali's rulers earned most of their riches by controlling trade routes. After Ghana fell, Muslim traders created different trade routes. To bring Muslim traders back, Sundiata built new trade routes. He used his army to keep the new and old routes safe from thieves.

Once again, the Muslim traders felt safe. They traveled on their old trade routes and paid tariffs to Sundiata for every load of goods they carried into or out of Mali.

The gold and salt trade was still very important. The gold from ancient Ghana mines was running out, but people in Mali found new mines. Muslim traders came to Mali to trade for this gold. The traders then traveled to Europe and Arabia and sold it. Most of the world used gold from Mali to make coins. Without Mali, other countries could not have made enough coins for their people to use.

Mali's rulers also controlled a large copper mine that added riches to the empire. Musa started a new trade route from this copper mine to Cairo, Egypt. The Malians traded copper bars for goods from the traders. The traders took the bars home and sold them to craftspeople who used the copper to make jewelry, cups, plates, and other things.

Enemies of Mali destroyed Timbuktu. Africans rebuilt the city. This is what it looks like today.

What Happened to Mali?

After Musa died in 1337, his son Maghan became king. Maghan was not a strong ruler like his father. Enemies took over the famous city Timbuktu. They set the mosques and schools on fire. Soon, other people began attacking the cities of Mali. The kingdoms Sundiata had joined together left the empire and began to rule themselves again.

By 1400, Mali had lost its central power and would never again be as strong. Over the next 200 years, the empire grew smaller and smaller until little more than Niani remained. Other kingdoms slowly began controlling the trade routes and fighting for power.

SONGHAY
EMPIRE   MOROCCO

AFRICA

Timbuktu
Kumbi Saleh
Gao

Jenne

Lake
Chad

LEGEND
Songhay Territory
Surrounding land
Cities
Water

N
W   E
S

Atlantic
Ocean

The Empire of Songhay

The largest ancient empire of West Africa was Songhay. It started around A.D. 800 when the Songhay people built Gao, the capital city on the Niger River. Early Songhay people were not powerful enough to fight their strong enemies. Mali took over Gao in 1325. After Musa died, the Songhay people fought and won their freedom.

Songhay grew stronger as Mali weakened. Songhay kings eventually took over what had been the lands of Mali to form the Songhay Empire. Each king fought wars that made the empire larger. At its height, the empire stretched to Lake Chad. A series of Songhay kings ruled the empire from 1464 to 1582.

WEST AFRICAN KINGDOMS TIMELINE

A.D. 700	The Soninke people start building Kumbi Saleh.
A.D. 800 to 1100	Ghana controls the gold and salt trade.
A.D. 1235	Sundiata unites kingdoms and forms Mali.
A.D. 1235 to 1500	Mali rules trade routes.
A.D. 1312	Mansa Musa becomes king of Mali.
A.D. 1324	Mansa Musa makes a pilgrimage to Mecca.
A.D. 1433	Enemies capture Timbuktu, and Mali grows weak.
A.D. 1464 to 1591	Songhay Empire controls trade routes.
A.D. 1591	Moors fight and defeat Songhay.

Songhay People and Government

The people of Songhay belonged to one of three groups. One group lived together in clans in the countryside. These people were farmers. Another group lived in the cities. These people were mostly traders, teachers, writers, and government workers. The third group sailed up and down the rivers in search of fish.

Songhay had several leaders, including King Askia. King Askia created the strongest central government in Africa at the time.

The Songhay Empire was too large to be controlled by just the army. So, kings divided Songhay into five parts called provinces. A governor was in charge of each province.

The kings also had a group of advisors. Advisors were in charge of the army, navy, farming, fishing, forests, and property. Each advisor had helpers. For example, the fishing advisor's helper kept track of the number of boats on the river.

All towns of Songhay had a Muslim mayor. The courts had Muslim judges, and they made decisions based on Muslim law.

The Songhay became rich through taxing traders who traveled along their trade routes. Besides this, all people paid tribute to the king. Songhay's families paid tribute, too.

Timbuktu

Timbuktu was an important trade city in the Songhay Empire. It was also a center for Muslim learning and culture. People came from as far as India to study in Timbuktu's schools. Merchants recorded in their writings that people in Timbuktu paid more money for books than they did for any other kind of goods.

The poor of Timbuktu lived in simple, round clay huts. The huts were close together on the sides of narrow streets. Rich merchants and traders lived in brick houses with two or more levels. Large mosques, which were also schools, dotted the city.

What Happened to Songhay?

Wars with the Moors ended the Songhay Empire. Moors are people from Morocco, a country in northern Africa. The Moors wanted West Africa's gold. The Songhay fought with iron spears, but the Moors fought with cannons and guns. Songhay's weapons were not strong enough. They lost the war.

These are the remains of a fortress soldiers used to protect the trade routes.

The Moors could not find the gold mines. Instead, they robbed the Songhay people and tore down many of their towns.

The wars left the Songhay Empire poor and divided. Its people could not run the salt and gold mines, and thieves robbed the traders.

No large empire took Songhay's place. After so many rich years, West African kingdoms lost control of the trade routes forever.

Allah (AH-lah)—the one god of Islam

ancient (AYN-shunt)—very old

artifact (ART-uh-fakt)—an object that was made or used by humans in the past

caravan (KARE-uh-van)—a group of travelers people who travel across a desert

clan (KLAN)—a group of people with a common family member

descended (di-SEND-ed)—to belong to a later generation of the same family

empire (EM-pire)—a group of countries with one ruler

epic (EP-ik)—a long story or poem about the adventures and battles of a king, god, or hero

griot (GREE-oh)—aan African historian and storyteller

local (LOH-kuhl)—something that is close to or from the neighborhood where you live

mansa (man-SAH)—a king of Mali

Mecca (MEK-ah)—a holy city of Islam

mosque (MAHSK)—a Muslim building of worship

Muslim (MUSH-lim)—a follower of Islam

organized (OR-guh-nized)—something that is planned and run well

pilgrimage (PIL-gruh-mij)—a trip for a religion reason

pottery (POT-ur-ee)—objects made of clay, such as pots, bowls, vases, and cups

priest (PREEST)—men who served the gods and worked in temples

route (ROWT)—a path to travel on

subject (SUHB-jikt)—a person who lives in an empire or kingdom

tariff (TA-rif)—a tax charged on goods that are brought into or carried out of a country

tribute (TRIB-yoot)—payment made by a group of people to their ruler

Africa: Cradle of Civilization
http://library.thinkquest.org/C002739/index2.
shtm

Ancient Africa
http://www.penncharter.com/Student/africa

Ancient Africa in the Electronic Passport
http://www.mrdowling.com/609ancafr.html

Ancient Africa's Black Kingdoms
http://www.homestead.com/wysinger/ancient
africa1.html

Civilizations in Africa
http://www.wsu.edu:8080/~dee/CIVAFRCA/CIV
AFRCA.HTM

Useful Addresses

The Africa Society
3511 North Street
Arlington, Virginia 22201-4907

**Berkeley Stanford Joint Center for
  African Studies**
356 Stephens Hall MC2314
Berkeley, CA 94720-2314

Center for African Studies
The Outreach Center
University of Illinois
910 South Fifth Street, Room 210
Champaign, IL 61820

Columbia University Institute of African Studies
Room 1103 SIPA
420 W. 118th Street
New York, NY 10027

Index